Weeknight Wonders

pil

Publications International, Ltd.

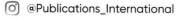

Let's get social!

@Publications_International

@PublicationsInternational

www.pilbooks.com

Breakfast for Dinner

Bacon and Potato Frittata
MAKES 4 TO 6 SERVINGS

5 eggs

½ cup bacon, crisp-cooked and crumbled

¼ cup half-and-half or milk

⅛ teaspoon salt

⅛ teaspoon black pepper

3 tablespoons butter

2 cups frozen O'Brien hash brown potatoes with onions and peppers

1 Preheat broiler. Beat eggs in medium bowl. Add bacon, half-and-half, salt and pepper; beat until well blended.

2 Melt butter in large ovenproof skillet over medium-high heat. Add potatoes; cook and stir 4 minutes. Pour egg mixture into skillet. Reduce heat to medium; cover and cook 6 minutes or until eggs are set around edges (top will still be wet).

3 Transfer skillet to broiler. Broil 4 inches from heat source 1 to 2 minutes or until top is golden brown and center is set.

Morning Pizza Margherita

MAKES 6 SERVINGS

1 (12-inch) prepared pizza crust

3 slices bacon or turkey bacon

8 eggs

½ cup milk

1½ tablespoons chopped fresh basil, divided

¼ teaspoon salt

⅛ teaspoon black pepper

2 plum tomatoes, thinly sliced

½ cup (2 ounces) shredded mozzarella cheese

¼ cup (1 ounce) shredded Cheddar cheese

1 Preheat oven to 450°F. Place pizza crust on 12-inch pizza pan. Bake 6 to 8 minutes or until heated through.

2 Meanwhile, cook bacon in large skillet over medium-high heat until crisp. Drain on paper towel-lined plate. Crumble bacon when cool enough to handle. Drain off all but 2 teaspoons drippings from skillet.

3 Whisk eggs, milk, ½ tablespoon basil, salt and pepper in medium bowl until blended. Add to skillet; cook over medium heat until eggs begin to set around edges. Stir gently, allowing uncooked portions to flow underneath. Stir egg mixture every 1 to 2 minutes or just until eggs are set. Remove from heat.

4 Arrange tomato slices on warm pizza crust; top with scrambled eggs, bacon and cheeses. Bake 1 minute or until cheeses are melted. Sprinkle with remaining 1 tablespoon basil. Cut into wedges; serve immediately.

Breakfast Migas

MAKES 6 SERVINGS

1 tablespoon olive oil

1 small onion, chopped

1 jalapeño pepper,* seeded and diced

3 corn tortillas, cut into 1-inch pieces

1 medium tomato, halved, seeded and diced

6 eggs

2 tablespoons chunky salsa

1 cup (4 ounces) shredded Monterey Jack cheese

1 small ripe avocado, diced

1 tablespoon lime juice

Jalapeño peppers can sting and irritate the skin, so wear rubber gloves when handling peppers and do not touch your eyes.

1 Heat oil in large nonstick skillet over medium heat. Add onion and jalapeño; cook and stir 2 minutes or until vegetables are softened.

2 Add tortillas and tomato; cook about 2 minutes or until soft and heated through.

3 Lightly beat eggs and salsa in small bowl. Pour into skillet; cook until eggs are firmly scrambled, stirring occasionally.

4 Remove skillet from heat; stir in cheese. Top each serving with avocado tossed in lime juice.

Note

Migas, a Mexican breakfast dish, is traditionally made with leftover tortillas that are torn into small pieces by hand.

Pecan Waffles

MAKES 8 WAFFLES

2¼ cups all-purpose flour

3 tablespoons sugar

1 tablespoon baking powder

½ teaspoon salt

2 cups milk

2 eggs, beaten

¼ cup vegetable oil

¾ cup chopped pecans, toasted*

Butter and maple syrup for serving

To toast pecans, cook in small skillet over medium heat 3 to 4 minutes or until lightly browned, stirring frequently.

1 Preheat classic round waffle iron; grease lightly.

2 Combine flour, sugar, baking powder and salt in large bowl. Whisk milk, eggs and oil in medium bowl until well blended. Add to flour mixture; stir just until blended. Stir in pecans.

3 For each waffle, pour about ½ cup batter into waffle iron. Close lid and bake until steaming stops. Serve with butter and maple syrup.

Cheesy Quichettes

MAKES 12 QUICHETTES

12 slices bacon, crisp-cooked and chopped

6 eggs, beaten

¼ cup whole milk

1½ cups thawed frozen shredded hash brown potatoes, squeezed dry

¼ cup chopped fresh parsley

½ teaspoon salt

1½ cups (6 ounces) shredded Mexican cheese blend with jalapeño peppers

1 Preheat oven to 400°F. Spray 12 standard (2½-inch) muffin cups with nonstick cooking spray.

2 Divide bacon evenly among prepared muffin cups. Whisk eggs and milk in medium bowl until blended. Add potatoes, parsley and salt; mix well. Spoon mixture evenly into muffin cups.

3 Bake 15 minutes or until knife inserted into centers comes out almost clean. Sprinkle with cheese; let stand 3 minutes or until cheese is melted. (Egg mixture will continue to cook while standing.*) Gently run knife around edges and lift out with fork.

Standing also allows for easier removal of quichettes from pan.

Bratwurst Breakfast Skillet

MAKES 4 SERVINGS

1½ pounds red potatoes

3 bratwurst links (about 12 ounces), cut into ½-inch slices

2 tablespoons butter

1½ teaspoons caraway seeds

4 cups shredded red cabbage

1 Cut potatoes into ¼- to ½-inch pieces; place in microwavable baking dish. Cover and microwave on HIGH 3 minutes; stir. Microwave 2 minutes or just until potatoes are tender.

2 Meanwhile, cook sausage in large skillet over medium-high heat 8 minutes or until browned and cooked through. Remove to paper towel-lined plate. Drain off drippings.

3 Melt butter in same skillet. Add potatoes and caraway seeds; cook 6 to 8 minutes or until potatoes are golden and tender, stirring occasionally. Return bratwurst to skillet; stir in cabbage. Cover and cook 3 minutes or until cabbage is slightly wilted. Uncover; cook and stir 3 to 4 minutes or just until cabbage is tender.

Ham and Vegetable Omelet

MAKES 2 TO 4 SERVINGS

6 eggs

¼ teaspoon salt

⅛ teaspoon black pepper

1 tablespoon vegetable oil, divided

2 ounces diced ham (about ½ cup)

1 small onion, diced

½ medium green bell pepper, diced

½ medium red bell pepper, diced

2 cloves garlic, minced

½ cup (2 ounces) shredded Colby cheese, divided

1 medium tomato, chopped

Hot pepper sauce (optional)

1 Whisk eggs, salt and black pepper in small bowl until blended.

2 Heat half of oil in large nonstick skillet over medium-high heat. Add ham, onion, bell peppers and garlic; cook and stir 5 minutes or until vegetables are crisp-tender. Transfer to medium bowl.

3 Wipe out skillet with paper towels; add remaining oil and heat over medium-high heat. Pour egg mixture into skillet; cook 2 minutes or until bottom is set, lifting edge of egg with spatula to allow uncooked portion to flow underneath. Reduce heat to medium-low; cover and cook 4 minutes or until top is set.

4 Gently slide omelet onto large serving plate; spoon ham mixture down center. Sprinkle with ¼ cup cheese. Carefully fold two sides of omelet over ham mixture; sprinkle with remaining ¼ cup cheese and tomato. Cut into four wedges; serve immediately with hot pepper sauce, if desired.

Cornmeal Pancakes

MAKES 4 SERVINGS

1½ cups yellow cornmeal

¾ cup all-purpose flour

1½ teaspoons baking powder

1 teaspoon salt

1⅓ cups plain Greek yogurt

⅔ cup milk

2 eggs, lightly beaten

¼ cup sugar

2 tablespoons plus 2 teaspoons butter, melted, divided

Optional toppings: fresh blueberries, additional butter and maple syrup

1 Combine cornmeal, flour, baking powder and salt in medium bowl; mix well. Whisk yogurt, milk, eggs, sugar and 2 tablespoons butter in large bowl until well blended. Stir in cornmeal mixture; let stand 5 minutes.

2 Brush griddle or large skillet with 1 teaspoon butter; heat over medium heat. Drop batter by ⅓ cupfuls onto griddle; cook 3 minutes or until tops of pancakes are bubbly and appear dry. Turn pancakes; cook 2 minutes or until bottoms are golden, adding remaining 1 teaspoon butter as needed. Serve with blueberries, additional butter and maple syrup, if desired.

Quinoa Breakfast "Fried Rice"

MAKES 4 SERVINGS

1 cup uncooked quinoa

1½ cups water

2 tablespoons vegetable oil, divided

1 carrot, finely diced

¾ cup frozen peas

4 ounces deli ham, finely diced (optional)

2 green onions, thinly sliced

2 teaspoons minced garlic

1 teaspoon grated ginger

3 eggs, lightly beaten

⅛ teaspoon coarse salt

1 tablespoon soy sauce, plus additional for serving

1 tablespoon ketchup

¼ teaspoon freshly ground black pepper

1 Place quinoa in fine-mesh strainer; rinse well under cold running water. Combine quinoa and 1½ cups water in large saucepan; bring to a boil over medium-high heat. Reduce heat to low; cover and cook about 15 minutes or until quinoa is tender and water is absorbed. Spread on baking sheet; cool completely.

2 Heat 1 tablespoon oil in large nonstick skillet over medium-high heat. Add carrot and peas; cook and stir about 4 minutes or until softened. Add ham, if desired; cook 2 minutes or until lightly browned, stirring occasionally. Add green onions, garlic and ginger; cook and stir 1 minute or until fragrant. Transfer to large bowl.

3 Add remaining 1 tablespoon oil to skillet; heat over medium-high heat. Add eggs and salt; cook and stir about 1 minute or until lightly scrambled and set. Break up eggs into small, bite-sized pieces with spatula.

4 Return carrot mixture to skillet. Add quinoa; cook and stir 2 minutes. Add 1 tablespoon soy sauce, ketchup and pepper; cook and stir 1 minute or until heated through. Serve with additional soy sauce, if desired.

Tip

Prepare the quinoa the night before and refrigerate. Then, begin with step 2 for an even quicker dinner.

Whole Grain French Toast

MAKES 4 SERVINGS

2 eggs

¼ cup milk

½ teaspoon ground cinnamon

¼ teaspoon ground nutmeg

2 tablespoons butter

8 slices whole wheat or multigrain bread

⅓ cup pure maple syrup

1 cup fresh blueberries

Powdered sugar (optional)

1 Preheat oven to 400°F. Spray baking sheet with nonstick cooking spray.

2 Whisk eggs, milk, cinnamon and nutmeg in shallow bowl until well blended. Melt ½ tablespoon butter in large nonstick skillet over medium heat. Working with two slices at a time, dip each bread slice in milk mixture, turning to coat both sides. Let excess egg mixture drip back into bowl. Cook bread slices 2 minutes per side or until golden brown. Transfer to prepared baking sheet. Repeat with remaining butter, bread and egg mixture.

3 Bake 5 to 6 minutes or until heated through.

4 Pour maple syrup into small microwavable bowl; microwave on HIGH 30 seconds or until bubbly. Stir in blueberries. Serve French toast topped with blueberry mixture; sprinkle with powdered sugar, if desired.

Ham and Egg Breakfast Panini

MAKES 4 SANDWICHES

1 tablespoon olive oil

½ cup chopped green or red bell pepper

¼ cup sliced green onions

2 slices (2 ounces) smoked deli ham, chopped

4 eggs

¼ teaspoon salt

⅛ teaspoon black pepper

8 slices multigrain or whole grain bread

4 slices (¾ ounce each) Cheddar or Swiss cheese

1 Heat oil in medium skillet over medium heat. Add bell pepper and green onions; cook and stir 4 minutes or until crisp-tender. Stir in ham.

2 Whisk eggs, salt and black pepper in small bowl until blended. Pour into skillet; cook 2 minutes or until egg mixture is almost set, stirring occasionally.

3 Heat grill pan or medium skillet over medium heat. Spray one side of each bread slice with nonstick cooking spray. Turn four bread slices sprayed side down; top each with cheese slice, one quarter of egg mixture and remaining bread slices, sprayed side up.

4 Grill sandwiches 2 minutes per side, pressing down lightly with spatula until toasted. (Cover pan with lid during last 2 minutes of cooking to melt cheese, if desired.) Serve immediately.

Southwestern Baked Omelet

MAKES 4 SERVINGS

1 tablespoon olive oil

2 large poblano peppers, cut into short, thin strips

1 large red bell pepper, cut into short, thin strips

8 eggs

½ cup milk

¼ cup all-purpose flour

½ teaspoon salt

¼ teaspoon baking powder

⅔ cup shredded sharp Cheddar cheese

½ cup picante sauce or salsa

½ cup sour cream (optional)

1 Preheat oven to 400°F.

2 Heat oil in large ovenproof nonstick skillet over medium heat. Add poblano peppers and bell pepper; cook 5 to 6 minutes until peppers are soft, stirring frequently.

3 Whisk eggs, milk, flour, salt and baking powder in medium bowl until well blended. Sprinkle cheese over peppers in skillet; immediately pour egg mixture over cheese. Cook without stirring 1 to 2 minutes or until bottom of omelet begins to brown. Transfer skillet to oven.

4 Bake, uncovered, 10 to 12 minutes or until omelet is set and knife inserted near center comes out clean. Let stand 5 minutes before cutting into wedges. Serve with picante sauce and sour cream, if desired.

Sweet Potato and Turkey Sausage Hash

MAKES 4 SERVINGS

2 mild or hot turkey Italian sausage links (about 4 ounces each)

1 tablespoon olive oil

1 large red onion, finely chopped

1 large red bell pepper, chopped

1 large sweet potato, peeled and cut into ½-inch cubes

½ teaspoon salt

½ teaspoon black pepper

¼ teaspoon ground cumin

¼ teaspoon chipotle chili powder

1 Remove sausage from casings; discard casings. Heat oil in large nonstick skillet over medium heat. Add sausage; cook and stir 3 to 5 minutes or until browned, breaking sausage into ½-inch pieces with spoon or spatula. Remove to plate.

2 Add onion, bell pepper, sweet potato, salt, black pepper, cumin and chili powder to skillet; cook and stir 5 to 8 minutes or until sweet potato is tender.

3 Stir in sausage; cook without stirring 5 minutes or until hash is lightly browned.

Breakfast Quesadillas

MAKES 4 SERVINGS

4 eggs

2 tablespoons milk

4 teaspoons vegetable oil, divided

1 can (4 ounces) chopped mild green chiles

8 soft corn tortillas

½ cup (2 ounces) shredded sharp Cheddar cheese

¼ cup chopped fresh cilantro

1 ounce pepperoni slices, quartered

1 Whisk eggs and milk in small bowl until blended. Heat 2 teaspoons oil in large skillet over medium heat. Cook eggs until set, lifting edges to allow uncooked portion to flow underneath. Remove to small bowl. Wipe out skillet with paper towel.

2 Spread 1 tablespoon chiles on half of each tortilla. Top with eggs, cheese and cilantro; sprinkle with pepperoni. Fold tortillas in half.

3 Heat remaining 2 teaspoons oil in skillet. Cook quesadillas in two batches 3 minutes per side or until cheese is melted.

Hearty Soups

Butternut Squash Soup

MAKES 4 SERVINGS

1 tablespoon olive oil

1 large sweet onion, chopped

1 medium red bell pepper, chopped

2 packages (10 ounces each) frozen puréed butternut squash, thawed

1 can (10¾ ounces) condensed reduced-sodium chicken broth, undiluted

¼ teaspoon ground nutmeg

⅛ teaspoon white pepper

½ cup half-and-half

1 Heat oil in large saucepan over medium-high heat. Add onion and bell pepper; cook 5 minutes, stirring occasionally. Add squash, broth, nutmeg and white pepper; bring to a boil over high heat. Reduce heat to low; cover and simmer 15 minutes or until vegetables are very tender.

2 Blend soup in saucepan with hand-held immersion blender or in batches in food processor or blender until smooth. Return soup to saucepan.

3 Stir in half-and-half; heat through. Add additional half-and-half, if necessary, to thin soup to desired consistency.

New England Clam Chowder

MAKES 2 SERVINGS

1 can (5 ounces)
   whole baby clams,
   undrained
1 baking potato,
   peeled and
   coarsely chopped
¼ cup finely chopped
   onion
⅔ cup evaporated milk
½ teaspoon salt
¼ teaspoon white
   pepper
¼ teaspoon dried
   thyme
1 tablespoon butter

1 Drain clams, reserving juice. Add enough water to reserved juice to measure ⅔ cup. Combine clam juice mixture, potato and onion in medium saucepan; bring to a boil over high heat. Reduce heat to low; simmer 8 minutes or until potato is tender.

2 Add evaporated milk, salt, pepper and thyme to saucepan; cook and stir 2 minutes over medium-high heat. Add butter; cook 5 minutes or until soup thickens, stirring occasionally.

3 Add clams; cook 5 minutes or until clams are firm, stirring occasionally.

Speedy Meatball Soup

MAKES 4 TO 6 SERVINGS

1 package (15 to 18 ounces) frozen Italian sausage meatballs without sauce

2 cans (about 14 ounces each) Italian-style stewed tomatoes

2 cans (about 14 ounces each) beef broth

1 can (about 14 ounces) mixed vegetables

½ cup uncooked rotini pasta or small macaroni

½ teaspoon dried oregano

1 Thaw meatballs in microwave according to package directions.

2 Combine tomatoes, broth, mixed vegetables, pasta and oregano in large saucepan. Add meatballs; bring to a boil over medium-high heat. Reduce heat to medium-low; cover and cook 15 minutes or until pasta is tender.

Quick and Easy Ravioli Soup

MAKES 8 SERVINGS

8 ounces mild Italian sausage, casings removed

½ cup chopped onion

1 clove garlic, crushed

2 cans (about 14 ounces each) chicken broth

2 cups water

1 package (9 ounces) frozen mini cheese-filled ravioli

1 can (about 15 ounces) chickpeas, rinsed and drained

1 can (about 14 ounces) diced tomatoes with mild green chiles

¾ teaspoon dried oregano

½ teaspoon black pepper

1 cup fresh baby spinach

Grated Parmesan cheese

1 Cook sausage, onion and garlic 5 minutes in large saucepan or Dutch oven over medium heat, stirring to break up meat. Drain fat. Transfer sausage mixture to medium bowl.

2 Add broth and water to saucepan; bring to a boil over medium-high heat. Add ravioli; cook 4 to 5 minutes or until tender.

3 Stir in sausage mixture, chickpeas, tomatoes, oregano and pepper; cook 5 minutes or until heated through. Stir in spinach; cook 1 minute or until wilted. Sprinkle with cheese just before serving.

Vegetable Chicken Noodle Soup

MAKES 6 SERVINGS

1 cup chopped celery

½ cup thinly sliced leek
   (white part only)

½ cup chopped carrot

½ cup chopped turnip
   (optional)

6 cups chicken broth,
   divided

1 tablespoon minced
   fresh parsley

1½ teaspoons fresh
   thyme *or*
   ½ teaspoon
   dried thyme

1 teaspoon minced
   fresh rosemary
   leaves *or*
   ¼ teaspoon
   dried rosemary

1 teaspoon balsamic
   vinegar

½ teaspoon salt

¼ teaspoon black
   pepper

2 ounces uncooked
   wide egg noodles

1 cup diced cooked
   chicken

1 Combine celery, leek, carrot, turnip, if desired, and ⅓ cup broth in large saucepan; cover and cook over medium heat 12 to 15 minutes or until vegetables are tender, stirring occasionally.

2 Stir in remaining 5⅔ cups broth, parsley, thyme, rosemary, vinegar, salt and pepper; bring to a boil over medium-high heat. Stir in noodles; cook until noodles are tender.

3 Stir in chicken. Reduce heat to medium; cook until heated through.

Tuscan Bean, Tomato and Spinach Soup

MAKES 4 SERVINGS

2 cans (about 14 ounces each) diced tomatoes with onions

1 can (about 14 ounces) chicken broth

2 teaspoons sugar

2 teaspoons dried basil

¾ teaspoon Worcestershire sauce

1 can (about 15 ounces) small white beans, rinsed and drained

3 ounces baby spinach or chopped stemmed spinach leaves

1 tablespoon extra virgin olive oil

1 Combine tomatoes, broth, sugar, basil and Worcestershire sauce in large saucepan or Dutch oven; bring to a boil over high heat. Reduce heat to low; simmer, uncovered, 10 minutes.

2 Stir in beans and spinach; cook 5 minutes or until spinach is tender.

3 Remove from heat; stir in oil just before serving.

Sweet Potato and Ham Soup

MAKES 6 SERVINGS

1 tablespoon butter

1 leek, thinly sliced

1 clove garlic, minced

4 cups reduced-sodium chicken broth

2 sweet potatoes, peeled and cut into ¾-inch pieces

8 ounces ham, cut into ½-inch pieces

½ teaspoon dried thyme

2 ounces stemmed spinach, coarsely chopped

1 Melt butter in large saucepan over medium heat. Add leek and garlic; cook and stir 3 minutes or until tender.

2 Add broth, sweet potatoes, ham and thyme; bring to a boil over high heat. Reduce heat to low; simmer 10 minutes or until sweet potatoes are tender.

3 Stir in spinach; cook 2 minutes or until wilted. Serve immediately.

Kansas City Steak Soup

MAKES 6 SERVINGS

8 ounces lean ground beef

3 cups frozen mixed vegetables

2 cups water

1 can (about 14 ounces) stewed tomatoes

1 cup chopped onion

1 cup sliced celery

1 cube beef bouillon

½ to 1 teaspoon black pepper

1 can (about 14 ounces) beef broth

½ cup all-purpose flour

1 Brown beef in large saucepan over medium-high heat 6 to 8 minutes, stirring to break up meat. Drain fat.

2 Add mixed vegetables, water, tomatoes, onion, celery, bouillon and pepper to saucepan; bring to a boil.

3 Stir broth into flour in small bowl until smooth. Stir into beef mixture until blended. Bring to a boil. Reduce heat to medium-low; cover and simmer 15 minutes, stirring frequently.

Tip

If time permits, let the soup simmer an additional 30 minutes to allow the flavors to blend.

Pesto Tortellini Soup

MAKES 6 SERVINGS

1 package (9 ounces)
   refrigerated
   cheese tortellini

3 cans (about
   14 ounces each)
   chicken or
   vegetable broth

1 jar (7 ounces)
   roasted red
   peppers, drained
   and thinly sliced

¾ cup frozen green
   peas

3 to 4 cups packed
   stemmed fresh
   spinach

1 to 2 tablespoons
   prepared pesto

   Grated Parmesan
   cheese (optional)

1 Cook tortellini according to package directions; drain.

2 Meanwhile, bring broth to a boil in large saucepan
   or Dutch oven over high heat. Add cooked tortellini,
   roasted peppers and peas; return to a boil. Reduce
   heat to medium; cook 1 minute.

3 Remove from heat; stir in spinach and pesto. Garnish
   with Parmesan.

Pozole

MAKES 6 SERVINGS

1 large onion, thinly sliced

1 tablespoon olive oil

2 teaspoons dried oregano

1 clove garlic, minced

½ teaspoon ground cumin

¼ teaspoon salt

2 cans (about 14 ounces each) chicken broth

1 package (10 ounces) frozen corn

2 cans (4 ounces each) chopped green chiles, undrained

1 can (2¼ ounces) sliced black olives, drained

12 ounces boneless skinless chicken breasts, cut into thin strips

Chopped fresh cilantro (optional)

1 Combine onion, oil, oregano, garlic, cumin and salt in large saucepan or Dutch oven; cover and cook over low heat about 6 minutes or until onion is tender, stirring occasionally.

2 Stir broth, corn, chiles and olives into saucepan; cover and bring to a boil over high heat.

3 Stir in chicken. Reduce heat to medium-low; cover and cook 3 to 4 minutes or until chicken is cooked through. Sprinkle with cilantro, if desired.

Italian Fish Soup

MAKES 2 SERVINGS

1 cup meatless pasta sauce

¾ cup water

¾ cup chicken broth

1 teaspoon Italian seasoning

½ teaspoon salt

¾ cup uncooked small pasta shells

4 ounces fresh halibut or haddock steak, 1 inch thick, skinned and cut into 1-inch pieces

1½ cups frozen vegetable blend, such as broccoli, carrots and water chestnuts or broccoli, carrots and cauliflower

1 Combine pasta sauce, water, broth, Italian seasoning and salt in medium saucepan; bring to a boil over high heat. Stir in pasta; return to a boil. Reduce heat to medium-low; cover and cook 5 minutes.

2 Stir in fish and frozen vegetables; return to a boil. Reduce heat to medium-low; cover and cook 4 to 5 minutes or until pasta is tender and fish begins to flake when tested with fork.

Spicy Thai Coconut Soup

MAKES 4 SERVINGS

2 cups chicken broth

1 can (13½ ounces) light coconut milk

1 tablespoon minced fresh ginger

½ to 1 teaspoon red curry paste

3 cups coarsely shredded cooked chicken (about 12 ounces)

1 can (15 ounces) straw mushrooms, drained

1 can (about 8 ounces) baby corn, drained

2 tablespoons lime juice

¼ cup chopped fresh cilantro

1 Combine broth, coconut milk, ginger and curry paste in large saucepan; mix well.

2 Stir in chicken, mushrooms and corn; bring to a simmer over medium heat. Cook 5 minutes or until heated through. Stir in lime juice. Sprinkle with cilantro just before serving.

Note

Red curry paste can be found in jars in the Asian food section of large grocery stores. Spice levels can vary between brands. Start with ½ teaspoon, then add more as desired.

Picante Black Bean Soup

MAKES 6 TO 8 SERVINGS

4 slices bacon, cut
   into ½-inch pieces

1 large onion,
   chopped

1 clove garlic, minced

2 cans (15 ounces
   each) black beans,
   undrained

1 can (about
   14 ounces)
   beef broth

1¼ cups water

¾ cup picante sauce,
   plus additional
   for garnish

½ to 1 teaspoon salt

½ teaspoon dried
   oregano

   Sour cream

1 Cook bacon in large saucepan over medium-high heat until crisp, stirring frequently. Remove to paper towel-lined plate.

2 Add onion and garlic to drippings in saucepan; cook and stir 3 minutes.

3 Stir in beans with liquid, broth, water, ¾ cup picante sauce, ½ teaspoon salt and oregano; bring to a boil. Reduce heat to low; cover and simmer 20 minutes. Taste and adjust seasoning, if desired.

4 Top each serving with sour cream; sprinkle with bacon. Serve with additional picante sauce.

Minestrone Soup

MAKES 4 TO 6 SERVINGS

¾ cup uncooked small shell pasta

2 cans (about 14 ounces each) vegetable broth

1 can (28 ounces) crushed tomatoes in tomato purée

1 can (about 15 ounces) white beans, rinsed and drained

1 package (16 ounces) frozen vegetable medley, such as broccoli, green beans, carrots and red peppers

4 to 6 teaspoons prepared pesto

1 Cook pasta according to package directions; drain.

2 Meanwhile, combine broth, tomatoes and beans in large saucepan; bring to a boil over high heat. Reduce heat to low; cover and simmer 3 to 5 minutes.

3 Add vegetables to broth mixture; return to a boil over high heat. Stir in pasta; cook, uncovered, until vegetables are tender. Top each serving with about 1 teaspoon pesto.

Savory Seafood Soup

MAKES 4 SERVINGS

2½ cups water or chicken broth

1½ cups dry white wine

1 onion, chopped

½ red bell pepper, chopped

½ green bell pepper, chopped

1 clove garlic, minced

½ teaspoon salt

8 ounces halibut, cut into 1-inch pieces

8 ounces sea scallops, cut into halves

1 teaspoon dried thyme

Juice of ½ lime

Dash hot pepper sauce

Black pepper

1 Combine water, wine, onion, bell peppers, garlic and salt in large saucepan; bring to a boil over high heat. Reduce heat to medium-low; cover and simmer 15 minutes or until bell peppers are tender, stirring occasionally.

2 Add fish, scallops and thyme; cook 2 minutes or until fish and scallops turn opaque. Stir in lime juice and hot pepper sauce. Season with black pepper.

Tips

If halibut is not available, cod, ocean perch or haddock can be substituted. When buying fresh fish, store it tightly wrapped in the refrigerator and use it within 2 days of purchase.

Quick Chicken & Turkey

Sassy Chicken and Peppers

MAKES 4 SERVINGS

1 tablespoon Mexican seasoning*

4 boneless skinless chicken breasts (about 4 ounces each)

1 tablespoon vegetable oil

1 red onion, sliced

1 medium red bell pepper, cut into thin strips

1 medium yellow or green bell pepper, cut into thin strips

½ cup chunky salsa or chipotle salsa

2 tablespoons lime juice

Lime wedges (optional)

*If Mexican seasoning is not available, substitute 1 teaspoon chili powder, ½ teaspoon ground cumin, ½ teaspoon salt and ⅛ teaspoon ground red pepper.

1 Sprinkle seasoning over both sides of chicken.

2 Heat oil in large nonstick skillet over medium heat. Add onion; cook 3 minutes, stirring occasionally. Add bell peppers; cook 3 minutes, stirring occasionally. Stir in salsa and lime juice.

3 Push vegetables to edge of skillet. Add chicken to skillet; cook 5 minutes. Turn chicken; cook 4 minutes or until chicken is no longer pink in center and vegetables are tender.

4 Serve chicken over vegetable mixture. Garnish with lime wedges.

Easy Make-at-Home Chinese Chicken

MAKES 4 SERVINGS

3 tablespoons frozen orange juice concentrate, thawed

2 tablespoons water

2 tablespoons soy sauce

¾ teaspoon cornstarch

¼ teaspoon garlic powder

4 teaspoons peanut or vegetable oil, divided

2 carrots, sliced

1 package (12 ounces) frozen broccoli and cauliflower florets, thawed

¾ pound boneless skinless chicken breasts, cut into bite-sized pieces

Hot cooked rice

1 Combine orange juice concentrate, water, soy sauce, cornstarch and garlic powder in small bowl; stir until smooth.

2 Heat 2 teaspoons oil in large skillet over high heat. Add carrots; stir-fry 1 minute. Add broccoli and cauliflower; stir-fry 2 to 3 minutes or until vegetables are crisp-tender. Remove vegetables to medium bowl.

3 Add remaining 2 teaspoons oil to skillet; heat over medium-high heat. Add chicken; stir-fry 2 to 3 minutes or until cooked through. Push chicken to side of skillet. Stir cornstarch mixture; add to skillet and bring to a boil. Return vegetables to skillet; cook and stir until heated through. Serve over rice.

Tip

To cut carrots decoratively, use a citrus stripper or grapefruit spoon to cut 4 or 5 grooves into whole carrots, cutting lengthwise from stem end to tip. Then cut crosswise into slices.

Mexican Turkey Casserole

MAKES 4 SERVINGS

2 teaspoons vegetable oil

12 ounces ground turkey

1 can (about 14 ounces) stewed tomatoes

½ (16-ounce) package frozen bell pepper stir-fry blend, thawed

¾ teaspoon salt

¾ teaspoon ground cumin

½ cup (2 ounces) finely shredded sharp Cheddar cheese

2 ounces tortilla chips, lightly crushed

1 Heat oil in large cast iron skillet over medium heat. Add turkey; cook about 5 minutes or until no longer pink, stirring to break up meat.

2 Stir in tomatoes, bell peppers, salt and cumin; bring to a boil. Reduce heat to low; cover and cook 20 minutes or until vegetables are tender.

3 Sprinkle with cheese and chips.

Southwestern Chicken and Rice

MAKES 4 SERVINGS

1 teaspoon chili powder

1 teaspoon ground cumin

4 boneless skinless chicken breasts (4 ounces each), pounded to ½-inch thickness

2 teaspoons canola oil

2 cloves garlic, minced

2 cups diced zucchini or yellow squash

½ cup salsa

1 package (8½ ounces) cooked brown rice

½ cup (2 ounces) shredded Mexican cheese blend

¼ cup chopped fresh cilantro

1 Combine chili powder and cumin in small bowl; sprinkle over both sides of chicken.

2 Heat oil in large nonstick skillet over medium-high heat. Add chicken; cook 3 to 4 minutes per side or until chicken is no longer pink in center. Remove to plate.

3 Add garlic to skillet; cook and stir 30 seconds. Add zucchini; cook and stir 3 minutes. Stir in salsa; cook 2 minutes or until zucchini is crisp-tender. Stir in rice; cook until heated through.

4 Return chicken to skillet; top with cheese and cilantro. Cover and cook 2 to 3 minutes or until chicken is heated through and cheese is melted.

Chicken Piccata

MAKES 4 SERVINGS

3 tablespoons all-purpose flour

½ teaspoon salt

¼ teaspoon black pepper

4 boneless skinless chicken breasts (4 ounces each)

2 teaspoons olive oil

1 teaspoon butter

2 cloves garlic, minced

¾ cup chicken broth

1 tablespoon lemon juice

2 tablespoons chopped fresh Italian parsley

1 tablespoon capers, drained

1 Combine flour, salt and pepper in shallow dish. Reserve 1 tablespoon flour mixture for sauce.

2 Pound chicken to ½-inch thickness between sheets of waxed paper with flat side of meat mallet or rolling pin. Coat chicken with remaining flour mixture, shaking off excess.

3 Heat oil and butter in large nonstick skillet over medium heat. Add chicken; cook 4 to 5 minutes per side or until no longer pink in center. Transfer to serving platter; tent with foil.

4 Add garlic to skillet; cook and stir 1 minute. Add reserved flour mixture; cook and stir 1 minute. Add broth and lemon juice; cook 2 minutes or until sauce thickens, stirring frequently. Stir in parsley and capers. Spoon sauce over chicken.

Tuscan Turkey and White Bean Skillet

MAKES 6 SERVINGS

1 teaspoon dried rosemary, divided

½ teaspoon garlic salt

½ teaspoon black pepper, divided

1 pound turkey breast cutlets, pounded to ¼-inch thickness

2 teaspoons olive oil

1 can (about 15 ounces) navy beans or Great Northern beans, rinsed and drained

1 can (about 14 ounces) fire-roasted diced tomatoes

¼ cup grated Parmesan cheese

1 Combine ½ teaspoon rosemary, garlic salt and ¼ teaspoon pepper in small bowl; mix well. Sprinkle over turkey.

2 Heat 1 teaspoon oil in large skillet over medium heat. Add half of turkey; cook 2 to 3 minutes per side or until no longer pink in center. Remove to platter; tent with foil. Repeat with remaining 1 teaspoon oil and turkey.

3 Add beans, tomatoes, remaining ½ teaspoon rosemary and ¼ teaspoon pepper to skillet; bring to a boil over high heat. Reduce heat to low; cook 5 minutes.

4 Spoon bean mixture over turkey; sprinkle with cheese.

Barbecue Chicken Stromboli

MAKES 6 SERVINGS

1 rotisserie-roasted chicken* (2 to 2¼ pounds)

⅓ cup barbecue sauce

1 package (about 14 ounces) refrigerated pizza dough

1 cup (4 ounces) shredded Cheddar cheese

⅓ cup sliced green onions, divided

Or substitute 8 ounces roast chicken breast from the deli, chopped, for the rotisserie chicken.

1 Remove and discard skin from chicken. Shred chicken meat; discard bones. (You should have about 4 cups shredded chicken.) Combine 2 cups chicken and barbecue sauce in medium bowl; mix well. Cover and refrigerate or freeze remaining chicken for another use.

2 Preheat oven to 400°F. Lightly spray baking sheet with nonstick cooking spray. Unroll dough on baking sheet; pat into 12×9-inch rectangle.

3 Spread chicken mixture lengthwise down center of dough, leaving 2½ inches on each side. Sprinkle with cheese and ¼ cup green onions. Fold long sides of dough over filling; press edges to seal. Sprinkle with remaining green onions.

4 Bake 19 to 22 minutes or until golden brown. Let stand 10 minutes before slicing.

Greek Chicken

MAKES 4 SERVINGS

12 cloves garlic, unpeeled

3 pounds chicken thighs and drumsticks

4 tablespoons lemon juice, divided

3 tablespoons olive oil

2 tablespoons chopped fresh rosemary leaves *or* 2 teaspoons dried rosemary

¾ teaspoon salt

½ teaspoon black pepper

1 teaspoon grated lemon peel

1 Preheat oven to 375°F. Scatter garlic cloves in shallow roasting pan; arrange chicken over garlic. Combine 2 tablespoons lemon juice, oil and rosemary in small bowl; spoon evenly over chicken. Sprinkle with salt and pepper.

2 Bake 50 to 55 minutes or until chicken is cooked through (165°F). Remove to serving platter; tent with foil.

3 Squeeze garlic pulp from skins; discard skins. Place garlic pulp in roasting pan; add remaining 2 tablespoons lemon juice. Cook over medium heat, mashing garlic and scraping up browned bits from bottom of pan. Pour sauce over chicken; sprinkle with lemon peel.

Tip

Unpeeled cloves of garlic usually burst open while roasting, making it easy to squeeze out the softened roasted garlic with your thumb and forefinger. If the cloves have not burst open, simply slice off the end with a knife and squeeze out the garlic.

Jerk Turkey Stew

MAKES 4 SERVINGS

1 tablespoon
  vegetable oil

1 small red onion,
  chopped

1 clove garlic, minced

½ teaspoon salt

½ teaspoon ground
  ginger

¼ teaspoon black
  pepper

⅛ to ¼ teaspoon
  ground red pepper

⅛ teaspoon ground
  allspice

1 can (about
  28 ounces)
  diced tomatoes

3 cups diced cooked
  turkey

2 cups diced cooked
  sweet potatoes
  (½-inch pieces)

½ cup turkey broth
  or gravy

1 tablespoon lime
  juice

1 tablespoon minced
  fresh chives

1 Heat oil in large saucepan or Dutch oven over medium heat. Add onion and garlic; cook and stir 5 minutes. Add salt, ginger, black pepper, red pepper and allspice; cook and stir 20 seconds.

2 Stir in tomatoes, turkey, sweet potatoes and broth. Reduce heat to low; cook 15 minutes, stirring occasionally.

3 Stir in lime juice; cover and let stand 10 minutes. Sprinkle with chives just before serving.

Variation

Instead of sweet potatoes, add a diced cooked white potato, or serve the stew over cooked rice.

Easy Chicken Parmesan

MAKES 4 SERVINGS

1 tablespoon olive oil

4 boneless skinless chicken breasts

1 medium onion, chopped

1 small zucchini, sliced

1 jar (26 ounces) pasta sauce

½ teaspoon dried basil

½ teaspoon dried oregano

8 ounces fresh mozzarella cheese, cut into thin slices

¼ cup grated Parmesan cheese

Hot cooked pasta (optional)

1 Preheat broiler.

2 Heat oil in large ovenproof skillet over medium-high heat. Add chicken; cook 5 to 7 minutes or until browned on both sides. Add onion and zucchini; cook 5 minutes or until vegetables are softened. Stir in pasta sauce, basil and oregano. Top chicken with mozzarella slices.

3 Broil 6 inches from heat 5 to 7 minutes or until chicken is no longer pink in center and cheese is beginning to brown. Sprinkle with Parmesan; serve with pasta, if desired.

Chicken Mirabella

MAKES 4 SERVINGS

4 boneless skinless chicken breasts (about 4 ounces each)

½ cup pitted prunes

½ cup assorted pitted olives (black, green and/or a combination)

¼ cup or dry white wine or white grape juice

2 tablespoons olive oil

1 tablespoon capers

1 tablespoon red wine vinegar

1 teaspoon dried oregano

1 clove garlic, minced

1 teaspoon chopped fresh parsley, plus additional for garnish

2 teaspoons packed brown sugar

1 Preheat oven to 350°F. Place chicken in 8-inch baking dish.

2 Combine prunes, olives, wine, oil, capers, vinegar, oregano, garlic and 1 teaspoon parsley in medium bowl; mix well. Pour over chicken; sprinkle with brown sugar.

3 Bake 25 to 30 minutes or until chicken is no longer pink in center, basting with sauce halfway through cooking. Garnish with additional parsley.

Tip

For more intense flavor, marinate chicken at least 8 hours or overnight. Sprinkle with brown sugar just before baking.

Chicken Fried Rice

MAKES 4 SERVINGS

2 tablespoons
  vegetable oil,
  divided

12 ounces boneless
  skinless chicken
  breasts, cut into
  ½-inch pieces

  Salt and black
  pepper

2 tablespoons butter

2 cloves garlic, minced

½ sweet onion, diced

1 medium carrot,
  diced

2 green onions,
  thinly sliced

3 eggs

4 cups cooked
  white rice*

3 tablespoons
  soy sauce

2 tablespoons sesame
  seeds

*For rice, cook 1½ cups
white rice according
to package directions
without oil or butter.
Spread hot rice on large
rimmed baking sheet;
cool to room temperature.
Refrigerate several hours
or overnight. Measure
4 cups.

1 Heat 1 tablespoon oil in large skillet over medium-high heat. Add chicken; season with salt and pepper. Cook and stir 5 to 6 minutes or until cooked through. Add butter and garlic; cook and stir 1 minute or until butter is melted. Remove to small bowl.

2 Add sweet onion, carrot and green onions to skillet; cook and stir over high heat 3 minutes or until vegetables are softened. Add to bowl with chicken.

3 Heat remaining 1 tablespoon oil in same skillet. Crack eggs into skillet; cook and stir 45 seconds or until eggs are scrambled but still moist. Add chicken and vegetable mixture, rice, soy sauce and sesame seeds to skillet; cook and stir 2 minutes or until well blended and heated through. Season with additional salt and pepper.

Jalapeño-Lime Chicken

MAKES 8 SERVINGS

8 bone-in chicken thighs

3 tablespoons jalapeño jelly

1 tablespoon olive oil

1 tablespoon lime juice

1 clove garlic, minced

1 teaspoon chili powder

½ teaspoon black pepper

⅛ teaspoon salt

1 Preheat oven to 400°F. Line 15×10-inch sheet pan with foil; spray with nonstick cooking spray. Arrange chicken in single layer in prepared pan.

2 Bake 15 minutes; drain off liquid. Meanwhile, combine jelly, oil, lime juice, garlic, chili powder, pepper and salt in small bowl; mix well.

3 Turn chicken; brush with half of jelly mixture. Bake 20 minutes. Turn chicken; brush with remaining jelly mixture. Bake chicken 10 to 15 minutes or until cooked through (165°F).

Southwestern Turkey Stew

MAKES 4 SERVINGS

1 tablespoon
vegetable oil

1 small onion, finely
chopped

1 clove garlic, minced

2 cups chicken broth

2 cups smoked turkey
breast, cut into
½-inch pieces

2 cups frozen corn

1 can (about
14 ounces) diced
tomatoes

1 package (about
8 ounces) red
beans and rice mix

1 to 2 canned chipotle
peppers in adobo
sauce, drained
and minced

Chopped green
onion (optional)

1 Heat oil in large skillet over medium-high heat. Add onion and garlic; cook and stir 3 minutes or until onion is translucent.

2 Add broth; bring to a boil. Stir in turkey, corn, tomatoes, rice mix and chipotle peppers. Reduce heat to low; cover and cook about 20 minutes or until rice is tender. Let stand 3 minutes before serving. Garnish with green onion.

Variation

For a spicier stew, use 1 can (about 14 ounces) diced tomatoes with jalapeño peppers instead of the regular diced tomatoes.

Quick Chicken Quesadillas

MAKES 4 SERVINGS

4 boneless skinless chicken breasts

3 tablespoons vegetable oil, divided

½ teaspoon salt

1 large yellow onion, thinly sliced

8 (6- to 8-inch) flour tortillas

3 cups (12 ounces) shredded mild Cheddar or Monterey Jack cheese

Optional toppings: salsa, sour cream and/or guacamole

1 Flatten chicken breasts; cut into 1×¼-inch strips.

2 Heat 2 tablespoons oil in large skillet over high heat. Add chicken; cook 3 to 4 minutes or until lightly browned and cooked through, stirring occasionally. Season with salt. Remove to plate.

3 Add onion to skillet; cook and stir about 5 minutes or until translucent. Remove to plate.

4 Heat remaining 1 tablespoon oil in same skillet. Place 1 tortilla in skillet; top with one quarter of chicken, onion and cheese. Place second tortilla over filling; press down lightly. Cook quesadilla about 2 minutes per side or until browned and crisp. Repeat with remaining tortillas and filling. Cut into wedges; serve with desired toppings.

BBQ Chicken Skillet Pizza

MAKES 4 TO 6 SERVINGS

1 pound frozen bread dough, thawed

1 tablespoon olive oil

2 cups shredded cooked chicken*

¾ cup barbecue sauce, divided

¼ cup (1 ounce) shredded mozzarella cheese

¼ cup thinly sliced red onion

½ cup (2 ounces) shredded smoked Gouda

Chopped fresh cilantro (optional)

Use a rotisserie chicken for best flavor and convenience.

1 Preheat oven to 425°F. Roll out dough into 15-inch circle on lightly floured surface. Brush oil over bottom and side of large cast iron skillet; place in oven 5 minutes to preheat.

2 Combine chicken and ½ cup barbecue sauce in medium bowl; toss to coat. Remove hot skillet from oven; press dough into bottom and about 1 inch up side of skillet.

3 Spread remaining ¼ cup barbecue sauce over dough. Sprinkle with mozzarella; top with chicken mixture. Sprinkle with half of onion and Gouda cheese; top with remaining onion.

4 Bake about 25 minutes or until crust is golden brown. Sprinkle with cilantro, if desired.

Meaty Meals

Spaghetti and Meatballs

MAKES 4 SERVINGS

8 ounces uncooked multigrain or whole wheat spaghetti

12 ounces ground beef

4 ounces hot Italian sausage, casing removed

1 egg

2 tablespoons plain dry bread crumbs

1 teaspoon dried oregano

2 cups tomato-basil pasta sauce

2 tablespoons chopped fresh basil

Grated Parmesan cheese

1 Preheat oven to 450°F. Spray baking sheet with nonstick cooking spray.

2 Cook spaghetti according to package directions; drain and keep warm.

3 Meanwhile, combine beef, sausage, egg, bread crumbs and oregano in medium bowl; mix gently. Shape mixture into 16 (1½-inch) meatballs; place on prepared baking sheet. Spray tops of meatballs with cooking spray. Bake 12 minutes, turning once.

4 Pour pasta sauce into large skillet. Add meatballs; cook over medium heat 9 minutes or until sauce is heated through and meatballs are cooked through (160°F), stirring occasionally. Serve meatballs and sauce over spaghetti; sprinkle with basil and cheese.

Pork and Sweet Potato Skillet

MAKES 4 SERVINGS

2 tablespoons butter, divided

12 ounces pork tenderloin, cut into 1-inch pieces

½ teaspoon salt

¼ teaspoon black pepper

2 medium sweet potatoes, peeled and cut into ½-inch pieces (about 2 cups)

1 small onion, sliced

4 ounces smoked turkey sausage, halved lengthwise and cut into ½-inch pieces

1 small green or red apple, cut into ½-inch slices

½ cup sweet and sour sauce

2 tablespoons chopped fresh parsley (optional)

1 Heat 1 tablespoon butter in large nonstick skillet over medium-high heat. Add pork; cook and stir 2 to 3 minutes or until pork is no longer pink. Season with salt and pepper. Remove to plate.

2 Add remaining 1 tablespoon butter, sweet potatoes and onion to skillet; cover and cook over medium-low heat 8 to 10 minutes or until sweet potatoes are tender.

3 Add pork, sausage, apple and sweet and sour sauce to skillet; cook until heated through, stirring occasionally. Garnish with parsley.

Picadillo Tacos

MAKES 4 SERVINGS

12 ounces ground beef

1 cup chopped green bell pepper

1 teaspoon ground cumin

1 teaspoon chili powder

¼ teaspoon ground cinnamon

1 cup chunky salsa

2 tablespoons golden raisins

8 (6-inch) flour or corn tortillas, warmed

1 cup shredded lettuce

½ cup (2 ounces) shredded Cheddar cheese

1 medium tomato, chopped

1 Combine ground beef, bell pepper, cumin, chili powder and cinnamon in large nonstick skillet; cook and stir over medium heat until beef is browned.

2 Stir in salsa and raisins. Reduce heat to low; cook 5 minutes or until beef is cooked through, stirring occasionally.

3 Divide beef mixture evenly among tortillas. Top with lettuce, cheese and tomato.

Quick Jambalaya

MAKES 4 SERVINGS

1 package (about 9 ounces) ready-to-serve brown rice

1 tablespoon vegetable oil

1 cup chopped onion

1 small green bell pepper, diced

3 cloves garlic, minced

2 tablespoons all-purpose flour

1 can (about 14 ounces) diced fire-roasted tomatoes

1 cup chicken broth

1 package (9 ounces) fully cooked andouille sausage, cut into ½-inch slices

1 teaspoon dried thyme

¼ to ½ teaspoon hot pepper sauce or smoked hot pepper sauce (optional)

Sliced green onions (optional)

1 Cook rice according to package directions.

2 Heat oil in large saucepan over medium heat. Add onion, bell pepper and garlic; cook 5 minutes, stirring occasionally. Stir in flour; cook and stir 1 minute. Add tomatoes, broth, sausage, thyme and hot pepper sauce, if desired; bring to a boil over high heat. Reduce heat to low; cook, uncovered, 15 minutes or until vegetables are tender and sauce thickens.

3 Stir in rice or serve over rice. Sprinkle with green onions, if desired.

Chili Wagon Wheel Casserole

MAKES 6 SERVINGS

8 ounces uncooked wagon wheel or other pasta

1 pound ground beef

¾ cup chopped onion

¾ cup chopped green bell pepper

1 can (about 14 ounces) stewed tomatoes

1 can (8 ounces) tomato sauce

¾ teaspoon salt

½ teaspoon black pepper

¼ teaspoon ground allspice

½ cup (2 ounces) shredded Cheddar cheese

1 Preheat oven to 350°F. Spray 2½-quart casserole with nonstick cooking spray. Cook pasta according to package directions until al dente; drain well.

2 Cook beef in large nonstick skillet over medium-high heat 5 minutes or until no longer pink, stirring to break up meat. Drain fat. Add onion and bell pepper to skillet; cook and stir about 4 minutes or until vegetables are tender.

3 Stir in tomatoes, tomato sauce, salt, black pepper and allspice; cook 2 minutes. Gently stir in pasta. Spoon mixture into prepared casserole; sprinkle with cheese.

4 Bake 20 to 25 minutes or until heated through.

Spicy Chinese Pepper Steak

MAKES 4 SERVINGS

1 boneless beef top sirloin steak (about 1 pound), cut into thin strips

1 tablespoon cornstarch

3 cloves garlic, minced

½ teaspoon red pepper flakes

2 tablespoons peanut or canola oil, divided

1 green bell pepper, cut into thin strips

1 red bell pepper, cut into thin strips

¼ cup oyster sauce

2 tablespoons soy sauce

3 tablespoons chopped fresh cilantro or green onions

1 Combine beef, cornstarch, garlic and red pepper flakes in medium bowl; toss to coat.

2 Heat 1 tablespoon oil in large skillet over medium-high heat. Add bell peppers; stir-fry 3 minutes. Remove to small bowl. Add remaining 1 tablespoon oil and beef mixture to skillet; stir-fry 4 to 5 minutes or until beef is barely pink in center.

3 Add oyster sauce and soy sauce to skillet; cook and stir 1 minute. Return bell peppers to skillet; cook and stir 1 to 2 minutes or until sauce thickens. Sprinkle with cilantro.

Ham and Barbecued Bean Skillet

MAKES 4 SERVINGS

1 tablespoon
   vegetable oil

1 cup chopped onion

1 teaspoon minced
   garlic

1 can (about 15 ounces)
   kidney beans,
   rinsed and drained

1 can (about 15 ounces)
   cannellini or Great
   Northern beans,
   rinsed and drained

1 cup chopped green
   bell pepper

½ cup packed
   brown sugar

½ cup ketchup

2 tablespoons
   cider vinegar

2 teaspoons dry
   mustard

1 ham steak (½ inch
   thick, about
   12 ounces)

1 Heat oil in large skillet over medium-high heat. Add onion and garlic; cook and stir 3 minutes. Add beans, bell pepper, brown sugar, ketchup, vinegar and mustard; mix well.

2 Trim fat from ham; cut ham into ½-inch pieces. Add ham to skillet. Reduce heat to low; cook 5 minutes or until sauce thickens and mixture is heated through, stirring occasionally.

Simple Weeknight Chili

MAKES 8 SERVINGS

1 pound ground beef or ground turkey

1 small onion, chopped

1 can (about 28 ounces) diced tomatoes

1 can (about 15 ounces) black beans, rinsed and drained

1 can (about 15 ounces) kidney beans, rinsed and drained

1 can (about 15 ounces) chickpeas, rinsed and drained*

1 can (6 ounces) tomato sauce

1 can (4 ounces) chopped green chiles

1 to 2 tablespoons chili powder

Or substitute an additional can of kidney beans for the chickpeas.

1 Cook beef and onion in large saucepan or Dutch oven over medium-high heat until beef is cooked through, stirring to break up meat. Drain fat.

2 Stir in tomatoes, black beans, kidney beans, chickpeas, tomato sauce, green chiles and chili powder; bring to a boil. Reduce heat to medium-low; cook about 20 minutes, stirring occasionally.

Serving Suggestions

Serve chili over hot cooked macaroni, rice or split baked potatoes.

Shredded Pork Tacos

MAKES 6 SERVINGS

2 pounds boneless pork roast

1 cup salsa

1 can (4 ounces) diced mild green chiles, drained

½ teaspoon garlic salt

½ teaspoon black pepper

Corn or flour tortillas, warmed

Optional toppings: tomatillo salsa, chopped onion, chopped fresh cilantro, shredded cabbage, sour cream, lime wedges

Slow Cooker Directions

1 Combine pork, salsa, chiles, garlic salt and pepper in slow cooker.

2 Cover; cook on LOW 8 hours or until pork is tender. Remove pork to large plate; let stand until cool enough to handle.

3 Shred pork into bite-sized pieces; serve on warm tortillas with desired toppings.

Pizza Casserole

MAKES 6 SERVINGS

2 cups uncooked rotini or other spiral pasta

1½ pounds ground beef

1 medium onion, chopped

Salt and black pepper

1 can (about 15 ounces) pizza sauce

1 can (8 ounces) tomato sauce

1 can (6 ounces) tomato paste

½ teaspoon sugar

½ teaspoon garlic salt

½ teaspoon dried oregano

2 cups (8 ounces) shredded mozzarella cheese

12 to 15 slices pepperoni

1 Preheat oven to 350°F. Cook pasta according to package directions; drain.

2 Meanwhile, brown beef and onion in large ovenproof skillet over medium-high heat 6 to 8 minutes, stirring to break up meat. Drain fat. Season with salt and pepper.

3 Combine pasta, pizza sauce, tomato sauce, tomato paste, sugar, garlic salt and oregano in large bowl; mix well. Add beef mixture; stir until blended.

4 Spread half of mixture in skillet; top with 1 cup cheese. Repeat layers. Top with pepperoni.

5 Bake 25 to 30 minutes or until heated through and cheese is melted.

Italian Sausage and Vegetable Stew

MAKES 6 SERVINGS

1 pound hot or mild Italian sausage links, cut into 1-inch pieces

1 package (16 ounces) frozen vegetable blend, such as onions and bell peppers

2 medium zucchini, sliced

1 can (about 14 ounces) Italian-style diced tomatoes

1 can (4 ounces) sliced mushrooms, drained

4 cloves garlic, minced

¼ teaspoon salt

1 Brown sausage in large saucepan over medium-high heat 5 minutes, stirring frequently. Drain fat.

2 Add frozen vegetables, zucchini, tomatoes, mushrooms, garlic and salt to saucepan; bring to a boil. Reduce heat to medium-low; cover and cook 10 minutes. Uncover; cook 5 to 10 minutes or until stew thickens slightly.

Beef and Broccoli

MAKES 4 SERVINGS

1 pound beef tenderloin steaks

2 teaspoons minced fresh ginger

2 cloves garlic, minced

2 teaspoons vegetable oil

½ medium onion, halved and sliced

3 cups broccoli florets

¼ cup water

3 tablespoons teriyaki sauce

Hot cooked rice

1 Cut beef crosswise into ⅛-inch-thick slices. Toss beef with ginger and garlic in medium bowl.

2 Heat 1 teaspoon oil in large nonstick skillet over medium heat. Add half of beef mixture; stir-fry 2 to 3 minutes or until beef is barely pink in center. Remove to medium bowl. Repeat with remaining oil and beef. Add onion to skillet; stir-fry 2 minutes or until crisp-tender.

3 Add broccoli and water to skillet; cover and steam 3 to 5 minutes or until broccoli is crisp-tender.

4 Return beef to skillet. Add teriyaki sauce; cook and stir until heated through. Serve over rice.

Variation

Increase the vegetable content of the dish by adding 1 thinly sliced small red bell pepper, 1 cup trimmed green beans and/or ½ cup shredded carrot; stir-fry the vegetables with the onion in step 2.

Grilled Prosciutto, Brie and Fig Sandwiches

MAKES 2 SANDWICHES

¼ cup fig preserves

4 slices (½ to ¾ inch thick) Italian or country bread

Black pepper

4 to 6 ounces Brie cheese, cut into ¼-inch-thick slices

2 slices prosciutto (about half of 3-ounce package)

¼ cup baby arugula

1½ tablespoons butter

1 Spread preserves over two bread slices. Sprinkle pepper generously over preserves. Top with cheese, prosciutto, arugula and remaining bread slices.

2 Heat medium cast iron skillet over medium heat 5 minutes. Add 1 tablespoon butter; swirl to melt butter and coat bottom of skillet. Add sandwiches to skillet; cook over medium-low heat about 5 minutes or until bottoms of sandwiches are golden brown.

3 Turn sandwiches and add remaining ½ tablespoon butter to skillet. Tilt pan to melt butter and move sandwiches so butter flows underneath. Cover with foil; cook about 5 minutes or until cheese is melted and bread is golden brown.

Sausage and Pepper Skillet

MAKES 4 SERVINGS

1 pound bratwurst or Italian sausage links, cut into ½-inch slices

1½ cups sliced onions

1½ cups green bell pepper strips

1½ cups red bell pepper strips

1 teaspoon paprika

1 teaspoon caraway seeds

1 Heat large skillet over medium heat. Add bratwurst; cover and cook about 5 minutes or until browned and no longer pink in center. Remove to plate; tent with foil to keep warm.

2 Drain all but 1 tablespoon drippings from skillet. Add onions, bell peppers, paprika and caraway seeds to skillet; cook and stir about 5 minutes or until vegetables are tender.

3 Combine bratwurst and vegetables; mix well. Serve immediately.

All-in-One Burger Stew

MAKES 6 SERVINGS

1 pound ground beef

2 cups frozen Italian-style vegetables

1 can (about 14 ounces) diced tomatoes with basil and garlic

1 can (about 14 ounces) beef broth

½ teaspoon salt

2½ cups uncooked medium egg noodles

Black pepper

1 Brown beef in large skillet or Dutch oven over medium-high heat 6 to 8 minutes, stirring to break up meat. Drain fat.

2 Stir in vegetables, tomatoes, broth and ½ teaspoon salt; bring to a boil over high heat.

3 Stir in noodles. Reduce heat to medium; cover and cook 12 to 15 minutes or until vegetables and noodles are tender. Season with additional salt and pepper.

Serving Suggestion

Serve with breadsticks or Italian bread and a simple salad.

Easy Moo Shu Pork

MAKES 2 SERVINGS

1 tablespoon
    vegetable oil

8 ounces pork
    tenderloin, sliced

4 green onions, cut
    into ½-inch pieces

1½ cups packaged
    coleslaw mix

2 tablespoons hoisin
    sauce or Asian
    plum sauce

4 (8-inch) flour
    tortillas, warmed

1 Heat oil in large nonstick skillet over medium-high heat. Add pork and green onions; stir-fry 2 to 3 minutes or until pork is barely pink in center. Stir in coleslaw mix and hoisin sauce.

2 Spoon pork mixture onto tortillas. Roll up tortillas, folding in sides to enclose filling.

Note

To warm tortillas, stack and wrap loosely with plastic wrap. Microwave on HIGH 15 to 20 seconds or until hot and pliable.

Speedy Seafood

Quick Pasta Puttanesca

MAKES 6 TO 8 SERVINGS

1 package (16 ounces) uncooked spaghetti or linguine

3 tablespoons plus 1 teaspoon olive oil, divided

¼ to 1 teaspoon red pepper flakes*

1 tablespoon dried minced onion

1 teaspoon minced garlic

2 cans (6 ounces each) chunk tuna packed in water, drained

1 can (28 ounces) diced tomatoes

1 can (8 ounces) tomato sauce

24 pitted kalamata olives

2 tablespoons capers, drained

For a mildly spicy dish, use ¼ teaspoon red pepper flakes. For a very spicy dish, use 1 teaspoon red pepper flakes.

1 Cook spaghetti according to package directions; drain and return to saucepan. Add 1 teaspoon oil; toss to coat. Cover and keep warm.

2 Heat remaining 3 tablespoons oil in large skillet over medium-high heat. Add red pepper flakes; cook and stir until sizzling. Add onion and garlic; cook and stir 1 minute. Add tuna; cook and stir 2 to 3 minutes. Add tomatoes, tomato sauce, olives and capers; cook until sauce is heated through, stirring frequently.

3 Add sauce to pasta; stir until coated. Serve immediately.

Gazpacho Shrimp Salad

MAKES 4 SERVINGS

½ cup chunky salsa

1 tablespoon extra virgin olive oil

1 tablespoon balsamic vinegar

1 clove garlic, minced

8 cups torn mixed salad greens or romaine lettuce

1 large tomato, chopped

1 small ripe avocado, diced

½ cup thinly sliced unpeeled cucumber

½ pound large cooked shrimp, peeled and deveined

½ cup coarsely chopped fresh cilantro

1 Combine salsa, oil, vinegar and garlic in small bowl; mix well.

2 Combine greens, tomato, avocado and cucumber in large bowl. Divide salad among four plates; top with shrimp. Drizzle dressing over salads; sprinkle with cilantro.

Hot Crab and Cheese on Muffins

MAKES 8 SERVINGS

4 **English muffins, split**

1 **tablespoon butter**

3 **green onions, chopped**

⅓ **cup chopped red bell pepper**

8 **ounces fresh crabmeat, drained and flaked***

1 **cup (4 ounces) shredded Cheddar cheese**

1 **cup (4 ounces) shredded Monterey Jack cheese**

1 **to 2 teaspoons hot pepper sauce**

Two cans (6 ounces each) fancy crabmeat, drained, can be substituted for fresh crabmeat.

1 Toast English muffins in broiler or toaster. Place muffin halves on large microwavable plate.

2 Melt butter in medium skillet over medium heat. Add green onions and bell pepper; cook and stir 3 to 4 minutes or until vegetables are tender. Remove from heat; stir in crabmeat, cheeses and hot pepper sauce.

3 Spoon about ⅓ cup crab mixture onto each muffin half. Microwave on HIGH 2 to 3 minutes or just until cheeses are melted and crab mixture is heated through.

Blackened Shrimp with Tomatoes

MAKES 4 SERVINGS

1½ teaspoons paprika

1 teaspoon Italian seasoning

½ teaspoon garlic powder

¼ teaspoon black pepper

8 ounces (about 24) small raw shrimp, peeled (with tails on)

1 tablespoon canola oil

1½ cups halved grape tomatoes

½ cup sliced onion, separated into rings

Lime wedges (optional)

1 Combine paprika, Italian seasoning, garlic powder and pepper in large resealable food storage bag; mix well. Add shrimp to bag; seal bag and shake to coat.

2 Heat oil in large skillet over medium-high heat. Add shrimp; cook 4 minutes or until shrimp are pink and opaque, turning occasionally.

3 Add tomatoes and onion to skillet; cook 1 minute or until tomatoes are heated through and onion is softened. Serve with lime wedges, if desired.

Fish Tacos with Cilantro Cream Sauce

MAKES 4 SERVINGS

½ cup sour cream

¼ cup chopped fresh cilantro

1¼ teaspoons ground cumin, divided

¼ teaspoon salt

1 pound skinless tilapia, mahimahi or other firm white fish fillets

1 teaspoon garlic salt

1 teaspoon chipotle hot pepper sauce, divided

1 tablespoon canola or vegetable oil

1 red bell pepper, cut into strips

1 green bell pepper, cut into strips

8 corn tortillas, warmed

4 limes, cut into wedges

1 For Cilantro Cream Sauce, combine sour cream, cilantro, ¼ teaspoon cumin and salt in small bowl; mix well. Refrigerate until ready to serve.

2 Cut fish into 1-inch pieces; place in medium bowl. Add remaining 1 teaspoon cumin, garlic salt and ½ teaspoon hot pepper sauce; toss gently to coat.

3 Heat oil in large nonstick skillet over medium heat. Add fish; cook 3 to 4 minutes or until center is opaque, turning once. Remove to plate. Add bell peppers to skillet; cook 6 to 8 minutes or until tender, stirring occasionally.

4 Return fish to skillet with remaining ½ teaspoon hot pepper sauce; cook and stir just until heated through. Serve in tortillas with sauce and lime wedges.

Linguine with Clam Sauce

MAKES 4 SERVINGS

8 ounces uncooked linguine

2 tablespoons olive oil

1 cup chopped onion

1 can (about 14 ounces) Italian-style stewed tomatoes, drained and chopped

2 cloves garlic, minced

2 teaspoons dried basil

½ cup dry white wine or chicken broth

1 can (10 ounces) whole baby clams, drained, juice reserved

⅓ cup chopped fresh parsley

¼ teaspoon salt

¼ teaspoon black pepper

1 Cook linguine according to package directions; drain.

2 Meanwhile, heat oil in large skillet over medium heat. Add onion; cook and stir 3 minutes. Add tomatoes, garlic and basil; cook and stir 3 minutes. Stir in wine and reserved clam juice; bring to a boil. Reduce heat to low; cook, uncovered, 5 minutes.

3 Stir in clams, parsley, salt and pepper; cook 1 to 2 minutes or until heated through. Spoon over linguine. Serve immediately.

Creamy Shrimp and Vegetable Casserole

MAKES 4 SERVINGS

1 pound fresh or thawed frozen medium raw shrimp, peeled and deveined

1 can (10¾ ounces) condensed cream of celery soup, undiluted

½ cup sliced fresh or thawed frozen asparagus (1-inch pieces)

½ cup sliced mushrooms

¼ cup diced red bell pepper

¼ cup sliced green onions

1 clove garlic, minced

¾ teaspoon dried thyme

¼ teaspoon black pepper

Hot cooked rice or orzo (optional)

1 Preheat oven to 375°F. Spray 2-quart baking dish with nonstick cooking spray.

2 Combine shrimp, soup, asparagus, mushrooms, bell pepper, green onions, garlic, thyme and black pepper in large bowl; mix well. Transfer to prepared baking dish.

3 Cover and bake 30 minutes. Serve with rice, if desired.

Almond-Coated Scallops

MAKES 4 SERVINGS

2 tablespoons plus 2 teaspoons olive oil, divided

1 clove garlic, crushed

¼ cup coarse plain dry bread crumbs

2 tablespoons sliced almonds, chopped

1½ teaspoons grated lemon peel, divided

¼ teaspoon salt

Black pepper

8 jumbo sea scallops, cut in half horizontally (about 1 pound)

1 Heat 2 tablespoons oil in medium skillet over low heat. Add garlic; cook and stir 2 minutes. Remove from heat. Discard garlic.

2 Combine bread crumbs, almonds, 1 teaspoon lemon peel and salt on plate; season with pepper. Brush scallop slices with remaining 2 teaspoons oil. Press scallops into bread crumb mixture to coat both sides.

3 Reheat oil in skillet over medium-high heat. Cook scallops in batches 2 to 3 minutes or until golden brown. Turn and cook 1 to 2 minutes. Sprinkle with remaining ½ teaspoon lemon peel. Serve immediately.

Shrimp, Chickpea and Tabbouleh Pockets

MAKES 2 TO 4 SERVINGS

1 cup diced tomatoes

1 cup chickpeas,
     rinsed and drained

1 package (7 ounces)
     prepared
     tabbouleh*

4 ounces cooked
     small shrimp, tails
     removed, chopped

2 whole wheat pita
     bread rounds

**Prepared tabbouleh
can be found in most
grocery stores; it is
usually located near the
refrigerated hummus and
salsa. If you can't find
prepared tabbouleh, you
can use a 5- or 6-ounce
package tabbouleh mix
prepared according to
package directions.*

1 Combine tomatoes, chickpeas, tabbouleh and shrimp in medium bowl; mix well.

2 Wrap pita rounds in paper towel; microwave on HIGH 10 seconds. Cut pita into halves; fill with tabbouleh mixture.

Pasta with Tuna, Green Beans and Tomatoes

MAKES 4 SERVINGS

8 ounces uncooked whole wheat penne, rigatoni or fusilli pasta

1½ cups frozen cut green beans

4 teaspoons olive oil, divided

3 green onions, sliced

1 clove garlic, minced

1 can (about 14 ounces) diced Italian-style tomatoes, drained

½ teaspoon salt

½ teaspoon Italian seasoning

¼ teaspoon black pepper

1 can (12 ounces) solid albacore tuna packed in water, drained and flaked

Chopped fresh parsley (optional)

1 Cook pasta according to package directions. Add green beans during last 7 minutes of cooking time (allow water to return to a boil before resuming timing). Drain and keep warm.

2 Meanwhile, heat 2 teaspoons oil in large skillet over medium heat. Add green onions and garlic; cook and stir 2 minutes. Add tomatoes, salt, Italian seasoning and pepper; cook and stir 4 to 5 minutes.

3 Add pasta mixture, tuna and remaining 2 teaspoons oil to skillet; mix gently. Sprinkle with parsley, if desired. Serve immediately.

Roast Dill Scrod with Asparagus

MAKES 4 SERVINGS

1 bunch (12 ounces) asparagus spears, ends trimmed

1 tablespoon olive oil

4 scrod or cod fillets (about 5 ounces each)

1 tablespoon lemon juice

1 teaspoon dried dill weed

½ teaspoon salt

¼ teaspoon black pepper

Paprika (optional)

1 Preheat oven to 425°F.

2 Place asparagus in 13×9-inch baking dish; drizzle with oil. Roll asparagus to coat lightly with oil; push to edges of dish, stacking asparagus into two layers.

3 Arrange fish fillets in center of dish; drizzle with lemon juice. Combine dill weed, salt and pepper in small bowl; sprinkle over fish and asparagus. Sprinkle with paprika, if desired.

4 Roast 15 to 17 minutes or until asparagus is crisp-tender and fish is opaque in center and begins to flake when tested with fork.

Mediterranean Shrimp and Bean Salad

MAKES 4 SERVINGS

10 ounces large cooked shrimp, cut into bite-sized pieces

1½ cups grape or cherry tomatoes, halved

1 large shallot, minced

¾ cup canned chickpeas

¼ cup shredded fresh basil

½ teaspoon salt

¼ teaspoon paprika

¼ teaspoon black pepper

⅛ teaspoon dried oregano

3 tablespoons tomato or vegetable juice

1 tablespoon white wine vinegar

1 tablespoon olive oil

1 Combine shrimp, tomatoes, shallot, chickpeas and basil in large bowl; mix gently.

2 Combine salt, paprika, pepper and oregano in small bowl; mix well. Gradually stir in tomato juice until blended. Stir in vinegar and oil.

3 Pour dressing over shrimp mixture; toss gently to coat.

Adriatic-Style Halibut

MAKES 4 SERVINGS

1 large tomato, seeded and diced (about 1¼ cups)

⅓ cup coarsely chopped pitted kalamata olives

1 clove garlic, minced

4 skinless halibut or red snapper fillets (about 6 ounces each)

¾ teaspoon coarse salt

¼ teaspoon black pepper

1 tablespoon olive oil

¼ cup dry white wine or vermouth

2 tablespoons chopped fresh basil or Italian parsley

1 Preheat oven to 200°F. Combine tomato, olives and garlic in small bowl; mix well.

2 Season fish with ¾ teaspoon salt and ¼ teaspoon pepper. Heat oil in large nonstick skillet over medium heat. Add fish; cook 8 to 10 minutes or just until fish is opaque in center, turning once. Transfer to serving platter; keep warm in oven.

3 Add wine to skillet; cook over high heat until reduced by half. Add tomato mixture; cook and stir 1 to 2 minutes or until heated through. Season with additional salt and pepper. Spoon tomato mixture over fish; sprinkle with basil.

Stewed Okra and Shrimp

MAKES 4 SERVINGS

8 ounces okra

1 tablespoon canola or vegetable oil

½ cup finely chopped onion

1 can (about 14 ounces) stewed tomatoes, undrained, chopped

1 teaspoon dried thyme

½ teaspoon salt

¾ cup fresh corn kernels or thawed frozen corn

½ teaspoon hot pepper sauce

2 ounces cooked baby shrimp

1 Remove and discard tip and stem ends from okra. Cut okra into ½-inch slices.

2 Heat oil in large nonstick skillet over medium heat. Add onion; cook and stir 3 minutes. Add okra; cook and stir 3 minutes. Add tomatoes with juice, thyme and salt; bring to a boil over high heat. Reduce heat to low; cover and cook 10 minutes.

3 Add corn and hot pepper sauce; cover and cook 10 minutes. Add shrimp; cook and stir just until heated through.

Make It Meatless

Penne Pasta with Chunky Tomato Sauce and Spinach

MAKES 4 SERVINGS

8 ounces uncooked multigrain penne pasta

2 cups spicy marinara sauce

1 large ripe tomato, chopped (about 1½ cups)

4 cups packed baby spinach or torn spinach leaves (4 ounces)

¼ cup grated Parmesan cheese

¼ cup chopped fresh basil

1 Cook pasta according to package directions.

2 Meanwhile, heat marinara sauce and tomato in medium saucepan over medium heat 3 to 4 minutes or until hot and bubbly, stirring occasionally. Remove from heat; stir in spinach.

3 Drain pasta; return to saucepan. Add sauce; toss to coat. Top with cheese and basil.

Tex-Mex Black Bean and Corn Stew

MAKES 4 SERVINGS

1 tablespoon canola or vegetable oil

1 small onion, chopped

4 cloves garlic, minced

1 teaspoon chili powder

1 teaspoon ground cumin

½ teaspoon salt

1 can (about 14 ounces) fire-roasted diced tomatoes

¾ cup salsa

2 medium zucchini or yellow squash (or 1 of each), cut into ½-inch pieces

1 can (about 15 ounces) black beans, rinsed and drained

1 cup frozen corn

½ cup (2 ounces) shredded Cheddar or pepper jack cheese

¼ cup chopped fresh cilantro or green onion

1 Heat oil in large saucepan over medium heat. Add onion; cook and stir 5 minutes. Add garlic, chili powder, cumin and salt; cook and stir 1 minute.

2 Stir in tomatoes, salsa, zucchini, beans and corn; bring to a boil over high heat. Reduce heat to low; cover and cook 20 minutes or until vegetables are tender. Top with cheese and cilantro.

Kale, Mushroom and Caramelized Onion Pizza

MAKES 4 SERVINGS

1 package (about 14 ounces) refrigerated pizza dough

1 tablespoon olive oil

1 cup chopped yellow onion

1 package (8 ounces) sliced mushrooms

3 cloves garlic, minced

4 cups packed coarsely chopped kale

¼ teaspoon red pepper flakes

½ cup pizza sauce

¾ cup (3 ounces) finely shredded mozzarella cheese

1 Preheat oven to 425°F. Spray 15×10-inch jelly-roll pan with nonstick cooking spray.

2 Unroll pizza dough on prepared pan; press evenly into pan and ½ inch up sides. Prick dough all over with fork. Bake 8 to 10 minutes or until lightly browned.

3 Heat oil in large nonstick skillet over medium heat. Add onion; cook and stir 8 minutes or until golden brown. Add mushrooms and garlic; cook and stir 4 minutes. Add kale and red pepper flakes; cover and cook 2 minutes to wilt kale. Uncover; cook and stir 3 to 4 minutes or until vegetables are tender.

4 Spread pizza sauce over partially baked crust. Spread kale mixture evenly over sauce; top with cheese. Bake 10 minutes or until crust is golden brown.

Classic Macaroni and Cheese

MAKES 8 SERVINGS (ABOUT 8 CUPS)

2 cups uncooked elbow macaroni

¼ cup (½ stick) butter

¼ cup all-purpose flour

2½ cups whole milk

1 teaspoon salt

⅛ teaspoon black pepper

4 cups (16 ounces) shredded Colby-Jack cheese

1 Cook pasta according to package directions until al dente; drain.

2 Melt butter in large saucepan over medium heat. Add flour; whisk until well blended and bubbly. Gradually add milk, salt and pepper, whisking until blended. Cook and stir until milk begins to bubble. Add cheese, 1 cup at a time; cook and stir until cheese is melted and sauce is smooth.

3 Add cooked pasta; stir gently until blended. Cook until heated through.

Mediterranean Pita Sandwiches

MAKES 4 SERVINGS

1 cup plain yogurt

1 tablespoon chopped fresh cilantro

2 cloves garlic, minced

1 teaspoon lemon juice

½ teaspoon salt, divided

1 can (about 15 ounces) chickpeas, rinsed and drained

1 can (14 ounces) artichoke hearts, rinsed, drained and coarsely chopped

1½ cups thinly sliced cucumber halves (halved lengthwise)

½ cup shredded carrot

½ cup chopped green onions

4 whole wheat pita bread rounds, cut in half

1 Combine yogurt, cilantro, garlic, lemon juice and ¼ teaspoon salt in small bowl; mix well.

2 Combine chickpeas, artichoke hearts, cucumber, carrot, green onions and remaining ¼ teaspoon salt in medium bowl. Stir in yogurt mixture until well blended. Divide cucumber mixture among pita halves.

Pesto Pasta with Asparagus and Tomatoes

MAKES 4 SERVINGS

8 ounces uncooked thin spaghetti

8 ounces asparagus spears, cut into 2-inch pieces

1 medium tomato, chopped

1 jar (3½ ounces) pesto sauce

2 tablespoons olive oil

1 clove garlic, minced

½ teaspoon black pepper

¼ teaspoon salt

¼ cup grated Parmesan cheese

1 Cook pasta according to package directions, adding asparagus during last 3 minutes of cooking.

2 Meanwhile, combine tomato, pesto, oil, garlic, pepper and salt in large bowl; mix well.

3 Drain pasta and asparagus. Add to bowl with pesto mixture; toss gently to coat. Sprinkle with cheese.

Pan-Fried Polenta with Tomato-Bean Salsa

MAKES 4 SERVINGS

2½ cups chopped plum tomatoes

1 cup canned white beans, rinsed and drained

¼ cup chopped fresh basil

½ teaspoon salt

½ teaspoon black pepper

2 tablespoons olive oil, divided

1 package (16 ounces) prepared polenta, cut into ¼-inch slices

¼ cup grated Parmesan cheese

1 Combine tomatoes, beans, basil, salt and pepper in medium bowl; mix well. Let stand at room temperature 15 minutes.

2 Meanwhile, heat 1 tablespoon oil in large nonstick skillet over medium-high heat. Add half of polenta slices; cook about 2 minutes per side or until golden brown. Remove to platter; tent with foil. Repeat with remaining oil and polenta slices.

3 Spoon salsa over polenta; sprinkle with cheese.

Zucchini Pad Thai

MAKES 4 SERVINGS

1¾ cups water

3 tablespoons packed brown sugar

3 tablespoons soy sauce

2 tablespoons lime juice

1 tablespoon vegetarian fish sauce or Worcestershire sauce

4 tablespoons vegetable oil, divided

2 large zucchini, cut into thin strips

1 package (14 ounces) firm tofu, pressed and cut into cubes

2 eggs, lightly beaten

2 cloves garlic, minced

1 tablespoon paprika

¼ to ½ teaspoon ground red pepper

8 ounces fresh bean sprouts, divided

4 green onions with tops, cut into 1-inch lengths

½ cup coarsely chopped unsalted dry-roasted peanuts

Lime wedges

1 Combine water, brown sugar, soy sauce, lime juice and anchovy paste in small bowl; set aside.

2 Heat 1 tablespoon oil in large skillet over medium-high heat. Add zucchini; cook and stir 2 to 3 minutes or until crisp-tender. Transfer to large bowl.

3 Add 1 tablespoon oil to skillet; heat over medium-high heat. Add tofu; cook about 5 minutes or until browned on all sides, turning occasionally. Add to bowl with zucchini.

4 Heat skillet over medium heat about 30 seconds or until hot. Drizzle 1 tablespoon oil into skillet and heat 15 seconds. Add eggs; cook 1 minute or just until set on bottom. Turn eggs over; stir to scramble until eggs are cooked but not dry. Add to bowl with zucchini.

5 Drizzle remaining 1 tablespoon oil into skillet and heat 15 seconds. Add garlic, paprika and red pepper; cook and stir 30 seconds or until fragrant. Add zucchini, tofu, egg and sauce mixture; cook and stir 3 to 5 minutes or until zucchini is tender and coated with sauce. Stir in bean sprouts, green onions and peanuts; cook about 1 minute or until green onions begin to wilt. Serve immediately with lime wedges.

Meatless Sloppy Joes

MAKES 4 SERVINGS

Nonstick cooking spray

2 cups thinly sliced onions

2 cups chopped green bell peppers

2 cloves garlic, finely chopped

2 tablespoons ketchup

1 tablespoon yellow mustard

1 can (about 15 ounces) kidney beans, rinsed, drained and mashed

1 can (8 ounces) tomato sauce

1 teaspoon chili powder

Cider vinegar

4 sandwich rolls

1 Spray large nonstick skillet with cooking spray; heat over medium heat until hot. Add onions, bell peppers and garlic. Cook and stir 5 minutes or until vegetables are tender. Stir in ketchup and mustard.

2 Add beans, tomato sauce and chili powder. Reduce heat to medium-low. Cook 5 minutes or until thickened, stirring frequently and adding up to $\frac{1}{3}$ cup vinegar if dry. Serve on sandwich rolls.

Baked Gnocchi

MAKES 4 TO 6 SERVINGS

1 package (about 17 ounces) gnocchi

⅓ cup olive oil

3 cloves garlic, minced

1 package (10 ounces) fresh spinach leaves

1 can (about 14 ounces) diced tomatoes

1 teaspoon Italian seasoning

Salt and black pepper

½ cup grated Parmesan cheese

½ cup (2 ounces) shredded mozzarella cheese

1 Preheat oven to 350°F. Spray 2½-quart baking dish with nonstick cooking spray.

2 Cook gnocchi according to package directions; drain.

3 Meanwhile, heat oil in large skillet over medium heat. Add garlic; cook and stir 30 seconds. Stir in spinach; cover and cook 2 minutes or until spinach wilts. Add tomatoes, Italian seasoning, salt and pepper; cook 5 minutes, stirring occasionally. Gently stir in gnocchi. Transfer to prepared baking dish; sprinkle with cheeses.

4 Bake 20 to 30 minutes or until casserole is bubbly and cheeses are melted.

Hearty Vegetable Stew

MAKES ABOUT 7 SERVINGS

1 tablespoon olive oil

1 cup chopped onion

¾ cup chopped carrots

3 cloves garlic, minced

4 cups coarsely chopped green cabbage

3½ cups coarsely chopped unpeeled new red potatoes

1 teaspoon salt

1 teaspoon dried rosemary

½ teaspoon black pepper

4 cups vegetable broth

1 can (about 15 ounces) Great Northern beans, rinsed and drained

1 can (about 14 ounces) diced tomatoes

Grated Parmesan cheese (optional)

1 Heat oil in large saucepan over medium-high heat. Add onion and carrots; cook and stir 3 minutes. Add garlic; cook and stir 1 minute. Add cabbage, potatoes, salt, rosemary and pepper; cook 1 minute.

2 Stir in broth, beans and tomatoes; bring to a boil. Reduce heat to medium-low; cook 15 minutes or until potatoes are tender, stirring occasionally. Sprinkle with cheese, if desired.

Classic Fettuccine Alfredo

MAKES 4 SERVINGS

12 ounces uncooked fettuccine

⅔ cup whipping cream

6 tablespoons (¾ stick) butter

½ teaspoon salt

Generous dash white pepper

Generous dash ground nutmeg

1 cup grated Parmesan cheese

2 tablespoons chopped fresh Italian parsley

1 Cook pasta according to package directions. Drain well; cover and keep warm in saucepan.

2 Meanwhile, heat cream and butter in large heavy skillet over medium-low heat until butter melts and mixture bubbles, stirring frequently. Cook and stir 2 minutes. Stir in salt, pepper and nutmeg. Remove from heat; gradually stir in Parmesan until well blended and smooth. Return to low heat, if necessary; do not let sauce bubble or cheese will become lumpy and tough.

3 Pour sauce over pasta; cook and stir over low heat 2 to 3 minutes or until sauce is thickened and pasta is evenly coated. Sprinkle with parsley. Serve immediately.

Variation

For Chicken Fettuccine Alfredo, add 2 cups fully cooked chicken strips when adding the sauce to the pasta in step 3. Or use leftovers from a rotisserie chicken; shred into bite-sized pieces before adding it to the saucepan.

Pumpkin Curry

MAKES 4 SERVINGS

1 tablespoon vegetable oil

1 package (14 ounces) firm tofu, drained, patted dry and cut into 1-inch cubes

¼ cup Thai red curry paste

2 cloves garlic, minced

1 can (15 ounces) solid-pack pumpkin

1 can (14 ounces) coconut milk

1 cup vegetable broth or water

1½ teaspoons salt

1 teaspoon sriracha sauce

4 cups cut-up fresh vegetables (broccoli, cauliflower, red bell pepper and/or sweet potato)

½ cup peas

Hot cooked rice

1 Heat oil in large skillet over high heat. Add tofu; cook and stir 5 minutes or until lightly browned. Add curry paste and garlic; cook and stir 1 minute or until tofu is coated.

2 Stir in pumpkin, coconut milk, broth, salt and sriracha; bring to a boil. Stir in vegetables. Reduce heat to medium; cover and cook 20 minutes or until vegetables are tender.

3 Stir in peas; cook 1 minute or until heated through. Serve with rice.

Mexican Pizza

MAKES 8 SERVINGS

1 package (about 14 ounces) refrigerated pizza dough

1 cup chunky salsa

1 teaspoon ground cumin

1 cup canned black beans, rinsed and drained

1 cup frozen corn, thawed

½ cup sliced green onions

1½ cups (6 ounces) shredded Mexican cheese blend

½ cup chopped fresh cilantro (optional)

1 Preheat oven to 425°F. Spray 15×10-inch jelly-roll pan with nonstick cooking spray.

2 Unroll pizza dough on prepared pan; press dough to edges of pan. Bake 8 minutes.

3 Combine salsa and cumin in small bowl; spread over partially baked crust. Top with beans, corn and green onions. Bake 8 minutes or until crust is golden brown. Top with cheese; bake 2 minutes or until cheese is melted. Cut into squares; sprinkle with cilantro, if desired.

Szechuan Cold Noodles

MAKES 4 SERVINGS

8 ounces uncooked vermicelli, broken in half, or Chinese egg noodles

3 tablespoons rice vinegar

3 tablespoons soy sauce

2 tablespoons peanut or vegetable oil

1 clove garlic, minced

1 teaspoon minced fresh ginger

1 teaspoon dark sesame oil

½ teaspoon crushed Szechuan peppercorns or red pepper flakes

½ cup coarsely chopped fresh cilantro (optional)

¼ cup chopped peanuts

1 Cook noodles according to package directions; drain.

2 Combine vinegar, soy sauce, peanut oil, garlic, ginger, sesame oil and peppercorns in large bowl; mix well. Add hot cooked noodles; toss to coat. Sprinkle with cilantro, if desired, and peanuts. Serve at room temperature or chilled.

Szechuan Vegetable Noodles

Add 1 cup chopped peeled cucumber, ½ cup chopped red bell pepper, ½ cup sliced green onions and an additional 1 tablespoon soy sauce to the sauce and noodle mixture.

Mediterranean Eggplant and White Bean Stew

MAKES 4 SERVINGS

1 tablespoon olive oil

1 medium onion, chopped

1 medium eggplant (1 pound), peeled and cut into ¾-inch chunks

4 cloves garlic, minced

1 can (28 ounces) stewed tomatoes, undrained

2 bell peppers (1 red and 1 yellow), cut into ¾-inch chunks

1 teaspoon dried oregano

¼ teaspoon red pepper flakes (optional)

1 can (about 15 ounces) Great Northern or cannellini beans, rinsed and drained

⅓ cup grated Parmesan cheese

¼ cup chopped fresh basil

1 Heat oil in large saucepan over medium heat. Add onion; cook and stir 5 minutes. Add eggplant and garlic; cook and stir 5 minutes.

2 Stir in tomatoes, bell peppers, oregano and red pepper flakes, if desired. Reduce heat to medium-low; cover and cook 20 minutes or until vegetables are tender.

3 Stir in beans; cook, uncovered, 5 minutes. Top with cheese and basil.

Index

Index

Index

Index

Metric Conversion Chart

VOLUME MEASUREMENTS (dry)

⅛ teaspoon = 0.5 mL
¼ teaspoon = 1 mL
½ teaspoon = 2 mL
¾ teaspoon = 4 mL
1 teaspoon = 5 mL
1 tablespoon = 15 mL
2 tablespoons = 30 mL
¼ cup = 60 mL
⅓ cup = 75 mL
½ cup = 125 mL
⅔ cup = 150 mL
¾ cup = 175 mL
1 cup = 250 mL
2 cups = 1 pint = 500 mL
3 cups = 750 mL
4 cups = 1 quart = 1 L

VOLUME MEASUREMENTS (fluid)

1 fluid ounce (2 tablespoons) = 30 mL
4 fluid ounces (½ cup) = 125 mL
8 fluid ounces (1 cup) = 250 mL
12 fluid ounces (1½ cups) = 375 mL
16 fluid ounces (2 cups) = 500 mL

WEIGHTS (mass)

½ ounce = 15 g
1 ounce = 30 g
3 ounces = 90 g
4 ounces = 120 g
8 ounces = 225 g
10 ounces = 285 g
12 ounces = 360 g
16 ounces = 1 pound = 450 g

DIMENSIONS

1/16 inch = 2 mm
⅛ inch = 3 mm
¼ inch = 6 mm
½ inch = 1.5 cm
¾ inch = 2 cm
1 inch = 2.5 cm

OVEN TEMPERATURES

250°F = 120°C
275°F = 140°C
300°F = 150°C
325°F = 160°C
350°F = 180°C
375°F = 190°C
400°F = 200°C
425°F = 220°C
450°F = 230°C

BAKING PAN SIZES

Utensil	Size in Inches/Quarts	Metric Volume	Size in Centimeters
Baking or Cake Pan (square or rectangular)	8×8×2	2 L	20×20×5
	9×9×2	2.5 L	23×23×5
	12×8×2	3 L	30×20×5
	13×9×2	3.5 L	33×23×5
Loaf Pan	8×4×3	1.5 L	20×10×7
	9×5×3	2 L	23×13×7
Round Layer Cake Pan	8×1½	1.2 L	20×4
	9×1½	1.5 L	23×4
Pie Plate	8×1¼	750 mL	20×3
	9×1¼	1 L	23×3
Baking Dish or Casserole	1 quart	1 L	—
	1½ quart	1.5 L	—
	2 quart	2 L	—